Hackney

Marvelous Math Writing Prompts

300 Engaging Prompts and Reproducible Pages
That Motivate Kids to Write About Math—
and Help You Meet the New NCTM Standards!

by Andrew Kaplan

SCHOLASTIC
PROFESSIONAL BOOKS

NEW YORK • TORONTO • LONDON • AUCKLAND • SYDNEY
MEXICO CITY • NEW DELHI • HONG KONG • BUENOS AIRES

Edited by Jacqueline Glasthal
Cover design by Josué Castilleja
Cover art by Mike Moran
Interior design by Solutions by Design, Inc.
Interior illustrations by Mike Moran

ISBN: 0-439-21860-8

Table of Contents

Introduction

Why Write About Math?

When people think of math, they often think of communication through numbers and symbols, rather than words. Yet the National Council of Teachers of Mathematics (NCTM) considers the communication of math through writing so crucial that it specified this form of communication as one of its ten instructional "Standards" for the year 2000. Why is writing about math so important? The process of writing about math gives students opportunities to

* find out what they know and don't know about mathematical topics;

* articulate and clarify their thoughts about mathematical ideas and concepts;

* justify their problem-solving techniques and consider alternative approaches to problem solving;

* integrate new mathematical ideas into their thinking;

* correct misconceptions; and

* develop an appreciation of how math is used in their everyday lives, and thus gain motivation for learning more math.

In addition, when students write about math they provide teachers with important information about what they are learning, how they approach and assimilate new concepts, what concepts they need help with, and how they feel about math class and math in general.

How to Use This Book

Marvelous Math Writing Prompts contains a variety of writing prompts on a wide range of math-related topics. These prompts encourage students to think and then write about these topics in a number of different formats, from letters and journal entries to word problems and stories.

The prompts in this book are grouped into two parts. In Part 1, the prompts encourage students to write

Marvelous Math Writing Prompts   Scholastic Professional Books

about their math class and the topics they encounter in a school setting. For your convenience, these topics have been grouped into familiar strands, such as addition, subtraction, geometry, measurement, probability and statistics, and mental math. In Part 2, the prompts concern students' use of math in their everyday lives outside of school. Here, the prompts are grouped into such topics as math at home, math at play, and money math.

The topics in this book have been chosen to accommodate a wide range of mathematical and writing ability levels. Within each topic, the prompts included require varying levels of sophistication and confidence with skills. When working with younger students or students with limited writing know-how, you may wish to start with *Drawing Math*, a special feature in this book. *Drawing Math* provides students with an opportunity to use both pictures and words to restate and solve problems. Another good way to introduce a topic to students of any age or ability level is to use *Show What You Know...*, a second special feature. *Show What You Know...* gives students an opportunity to draw

on their prior knowledge of a given topic.

As with all good problem-solving techniques, there is more than one right way to use this book and the writing prompts contained within it. Sometimes, to stimulate interest, you may wish to give students a choice of topics. At other times, you may wish to assign a specific writing prompt geared toward a particular curriculum goal. Similarly, students may sometimes benefit from working cooperatively on a prompt or from sharing their responses within a class or small-group discussion. At other times, particularly when the prompts involve students' feelings and personal ideas, you may wish to give students the option of keeping their responses private.

Since the prompts in this book are designed to develop both mathematical *and* verbal skills, the mechanics of good writing, such as punctuation, complete sentences, spelling, and capitalization should be encouraged. However, to avoid inhibiting students' thought processes, you may wish to reserve a mechanics review until after students have had a chance to get their basic ideas down on paper.

Part 1:
Math in School

Students can feel empowered if given an opportunity to express what they are learning in their own words, as well as to share any ideas and opinions they have. Since math class is the place where students develop much of their math knowledge—from being introduced to new math skills and concepts to receiving practice applying these skills—it makes sense that this is also the place for them to ask questions about ideas they do not understand and to discuss their feelings about math. This process of learning, applying, and responding to mathematics is enhanced by writing about it. It allows students additional opportunities to record mathematical experiences, clarify understanding of mathematical concepts, and request additional information from teachers. For the math teacher, a student's writings about math provide a way to assess both the student's progress and the success of the teacher's instructional methods.

This section begins with students writing about math class. Students then write about a variety of core mathematical topics, from place value to problem solving, with a variety of other skills in between.

Marvelous Math Writing Prompts   Scholastic Professional Books

Let's Talk Math, Class!

DRAWING MATH

Directions: Draw a picture of your perfect math partner. Label all the skills and abilities that your perfect partner would have.

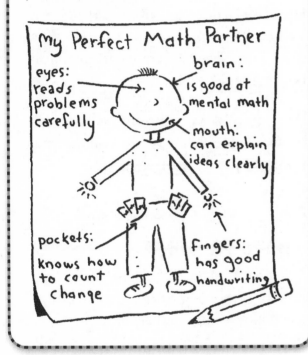

My Perfect Math Partner

eyes: reads problems carefully

brain: is good at mental math

mouth: can explain ideas clearly

pockets: knows how to count change

fingers: has good handwriting

Do you think you make a good math partner? Explain. Also tell what you can do to become a better one.

List three things you like and three things you don't like about working in a math group.

If you could change one thing about your math class, what would it be? Explain why you think your class would be better if this change were made.

Finish this sentence: "When I need help with math, I…"

List ten or more math facts you can use to describe your math class. For example, what is your room number? What shape is the room? How many desks are there? How many students have brown eyes? What other math facts can you think of to describe your class?

Explain how you use math in another school subject, such as history, science, music, or art.

Imagine that you are your own math teacher. List ten things that you want your students to learn by the end of the year.

Describe the way you are graded in your math class now. Would you like to be graded a different way? If so, describe it. If not, explain why you like the system used now.

Imagine that you are your own math teacher. Create a report card showing how you are doing in math. Include areas in which you are doing well, and others where you need improvement. Be as specific as you can.

Create a list of instructions titled "How to Get a Great Grade on Your Next Math Test."

Marvelous Math Writing Prompts   Scholastic Professional Books

How have math classes changed since your parents or grandparents were your age? Interview an adult to find out. Then write about it!

Write a letter to a friend describing what you did and what you learned in your math class today.

Describe a time when something you learned in your math class came in handy somewhere else.

Describe a time when you helped a friend solve a math problem. What was the problem? Explain how you helped.

Make a dictionary of important math words that you know. Put the words in alphabetical order, and define each one.

When you do math, do you check your work? Why or why not?

Write a silly story called "The Fish Who Loved Math Class." In the story, show why the fish loved math so much!

Describe what you think math classes will be like 100 years from now. What may be different? What will probably be the same?

Do you think you should be allowed to use a calculator when you do math homework? Why or why not?

MATH PROJECT

Help a younger child with math. Then write about what happened. Use these questions to help you:

❋ What math skill did you explain?

❋ How easy or difficult was it to explain this math skill? Why do you think that was?

❋ Did you use any teaching tools, such as models or drawings, to help you teach? If so, what did you use? Were these tools useful? Why or why not?

❋ Do you think you make a good math teacher? Why or why not?

Marvelous Math Writing Prompts Scholastic Professional Books

Name _____ Date _____

In Our Class, Math Really Adds Up!

Using the space below, create an ad for your math class or a favorite math skill. Start your ad with one of these slogans, or make up your own!

Numbers: You Can Count on Them!

Money Math: It Makes Good Cents!

Geometry: It's Not Just for Squares!

Fractions: They're Part of the Whole Picture!

Let Subtraction Make a Difference in Your Life!

Marvelous Math Writing Prompts Scholastic Professional Books

Numbers and Place Value

Show What You Know About...
Number Systems

Here are some ways that you can write the number five:

five	**5**	**V**
1 + 4	**卌**	

Can you think of others? Why do you think it is useful to be able to write a number in more than one way?

A unicycle is a vehicle with one wheel. What other words begin with the prefix "uni-"? How about the prefix "bi-"? The prefix "tri-"? What do you think each of these prefixes mean?

Suppose you had 68 pennies. How many piles of 10 could you make? Explain how you know.

How long do you think it would take you to count up to a million by ones? What makes you think so?

Explain why "place holder" is a good name for the zero in the number 406.

Do you think the following statement is true or false? *It would take just as long to count up to 100 by ones as it would take to count up to 200 by twos.* Explain your response.

Pick a number! Any number! On a sheet of paper, describe it as many ways as you can…without using the number or its name. Share the paper with a friend. Can he or she figure out what the number is?

Marvelous Math Writing Prompts Scholastic Professional Books

Write a silly story about No Number—a town where all the numbers were stolen one day. Describe how the people lived without numbers, and how they finally got the numbers back.

Name one or more places where you have seen Roman numerals used.

These number statements using Roman numerals are all true:

III = 3   VIII = 8

XI = 11   IV = 4

Using the true statements above, can you figure out what these Roman numerals stand for? Explain why you think so.

V = ?   X = ?   IX = ?

What does the symbol > stand for? How about the < symbol? How many other math symbols can you think of? What are they? Explain in a sentence or two what each means.

DRAWING MATH

Background: An abacus is an old counting tool still used in Asia. Each row of beads on it stands for a different place value. Each bead at the top of the abacus stands for five units. The beads at the bottom each stand for one unit. To show a number, move the beads toward the middle.

This abacus shows zero:

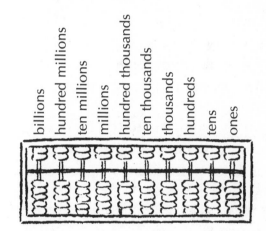

This abacus shows 263:

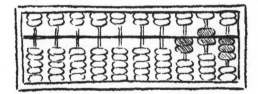

Directions: Draw an abacus showing another number. Then swap with a friend. Can you figure out what number your friend drew?

Marvelous Math Writing Prompts   Scholastic Professional Books

What's the largest number you can create by rearranging these digits:

8, 2, 4, 7, and 1

Explain why that is.

Explain what the 7 means in the number 2,743.

How would you write the following as a number: 8 thousand and 6 ones. Explain how you know.

When counting from zero, what's the first two-digit number you come to? Why do you think ten is so important in the number system we use?

Count up from one until you reach a number that has the letter "a" in it when it is spelled out. What is it? How did you figure it out? Can you think of any shortcuts you can use so that you don't have to spell out every single number to find out?

Imagine that you're speaking to a creature from outer space, who wants to know what "one hundred" means. How would you explain it?

Using words and pictures, describe three different ways you could solve the problem 14 + 12 = ?

Pick a number and write a poem about it, telling why you think it's so great.

What's the highest you ever remember counting? Describe what you were counting, and about how long it took.

Write a sentence in which you use both words in one of these homophone word pairs correctly:

one	won
two	to
four	for
eight	ate

How are the numbers 10 and 100 alike? How are they different?

In what ways is the number 10 like the number 16? How is it different?

Marvelous Math Writing Prompts   Scholastic Professional Books

List ten even numbers. Now list ten odd numbers. Describe how you know if a number is odd or even.

What is your address? What is the address next door? The address across the street? In what ways are the numbers on your side of the street all similar? How are they like the ones across the street? In what ways do they differ?

The numbers 1, 2, and 3 are consecutive numbers. So are the numbers 29, 30, and 31. Write a definition that explains consecutive numbers. Then write a sentence that has the word "consecutive" in it.

A digital clock shows the time 7:30. What time will it show 30 minutes later? Will a clock ever show the time 7:60? Why or why not? Explain.

Is the number $3\frac{1}{2}$ more than, less than, or equal to the number 3.5? Explain how you know.

List five or more places where you might see decimals, such as 3.15 or 0.66, used.

Pick any two consecutive numbers and add them. Now add a different pair of consecutive numbers. Will the answer always be odd or even? Explain why you think that is.

Pick any two even numbers and add them. Will the answer always be odd or even? Explain why you think that is.

Pick any two odd numbers and add them. Will the answer always be odd or even? Explain why you think that is.

Shown here are four palindrome numbers:

11   282   5,775   39,193

Figure out how all the numbers are alike. Then write a definition for palindrome.

What numbers can you think of that are between 2 and 3? Where are you likely to see numbers like these? When do you think they can come in handy?

List five or more places where you might see decimal-fractions, such as $\frac{1}{2}$ or $\frac{3}{4}$, used.

Name _____ Date _____

All Set to Do Math!

Imagine that each symbol below stands for a different number. List some of the number sets that would make the equation correct. Then describe on the back of this page any rules that you find to be true for all of these number sets.

$$\triangle + \square = \bigcirc - 2$$

$$\triangle + \square = \bigcirc - 2$$

$$\triangle + \square = \bigcirc - 2$$

$$\triangle + \square = \bigcirc - 2$$

$$\triangle + \square = \bigcirc - 2$$

14

Geometry

Show What You Know About...
Geometry

In what ways is a square similar to a cube? In what ways are they different? In what ways is a triangle similar to a pyramid? In what ways are they different? Describe other ways that solid shapes and flat shapes are alike. Then describe other ways that they differ.

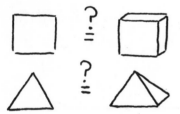

DRAWING MATH

Directions: Draw a scene of an imaginary place called ShapeTown. In your picture, use each of these shapes at least once:

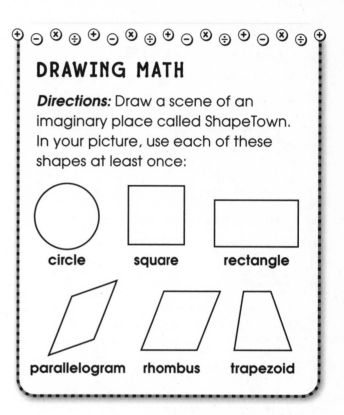

circle   square   rectangle

parallelogram   rhombus   trapezoid

Circles have no corners. Most coins are circle-shaped. How else can you describe a circle? How about a rectangle? A square?

Do you have a favorite shape? What is it? Why do you think you like it so much? Write a poem or a poster describing why it's so great.

What do rhombuses, rectangles, parallelograms, and trapezoids all have in common? Name at least one other shape you know that shares the same trait(s).

Describe how you could use a line segment to split one rectangle into two triangles. Then describe how you could use two line segments to split a rectangle into four triangles. What other shapes can you make from a rectangle, using just two line segments?

Marvelous Math Writing Prompts Scholastic Professional Books

Use these clues to find the mystery shape:

I have 2 short sides
    that are the same length.

I have 2 long sides
    that are the same length.

The sides that are opposite
    each other are parallel.

I have no right angles.

What shape am I?

Can you draw me?

Now create your own riddle for a different shape. Then challenge a classmate to figure out what shape you described.

Describe how a compass (like the one shown here) can be used to help you draw a circle.

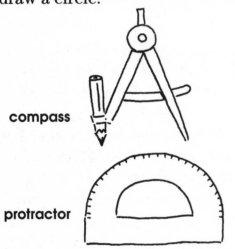

compass

protractor

In what ways are a protractor and a compass similar? In what ways are they different?

Describe one or more ways that you could use a sheet of loose-leaf paper to help you draw a square.

In your own words, explain the similarities and differences between area and perimeter.

Figure out how many different ways there are to arrange four square tiles. When you rearrange the tiles, do you change the shape's area? How about its perimeter? Explain.

What shape could you trace from a cone? Explain.

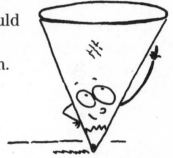

If you cut a baseball down the middle, what shape would you see inside? Explain.

If you cut a cereal box down the middle, what shape would you see inside? Would the shape change depending on how you cut the cereal box? Explain.

The capital letters A, B, C, D, E, H, and I are all symmetrical. Explain what symmetry means. Then identify other letters in the alphabet that are symmetrical. Explain how you know.

Marvelous Math Writing Prompts Scholastic Professional Books

Tell whether each of the following statements is true or false. Explain your answers:

1. All rectangles are squares.

2. All squares are rectangles.

3. Some rectangles are squares.

Imagine that you had a pile of softballs and a pile of blocks, and that all these items were about the same size. Which do you think your toy chest would hold more of: the balls or the blocks? Why do you think that is?

Which could you fit more of in a popcorn tub: popcorn or unpopped popcorn kernels? Explain why you think so.

Write a dialogue between a square, a circle, and a triangle in which each tries to prove to the others that it is the most important shape.

Explain the similarities and differences between a right triangle, an equilateral triangle, and a scalene triangle.

Imagine that you could fly to the ceiling and take a look at this structure from above. How many blocks do you think you would see? Explain why that is.

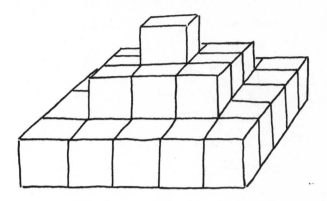

It's easy to find the center of a straight line segment by using a ruler. But can you think of a way to find the center point of a circle? Describe one idea of how this might be done.

Imagine that you could earn $1.00 for each side of a shape that you drew. Would it be worth more to draw a pentagon, a hexagon, an octagon, or a rhombus? Explain how you know.

What's the fewest number of sides that a regular shape can have? Explain why you think so.

List some items that you see every day that are shaped like circles. Make a separate list of items you see every day that are shaped like squares. Which do you think you see more of: circles or squares? Why do you think that is?

Can two shapes be congruent but not similar? Can two shapes be similar but not congruent? Explain.

Marvelous Math Writing Prompts Scholastic Professional Books

Name _____ Date _____

Pyramid Power

This is a pyramid:

Which of these drawings can you fold into a pyramid? How do you know? On a separate page, explain how the other figures would look when folded.

A.

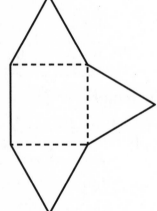

B.

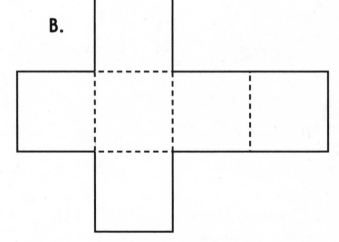

C.

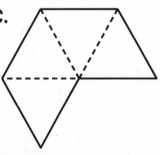

D.

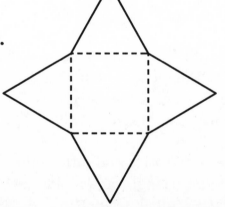

Building a Building

1. You'll need 8 cube-shaped items, such as number cubes, sugar cubes, or building blocks, to complete this activity. Using the cubes, see if you can create the structure described in the drawings below. Here's how:

   a. Each drawing below shows a different side of the same completed structure. The lighter areas in the drawings are close to you. The darker areas are farther away.

   b. Start with any one of the six drawings, and use the cubes to show how that side of the structure should look.

   c. Now add the other five sides, one at a time.

   d. When you're done, check your model. Each side should match the drawings.

Left Side

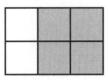
Front

Right Side

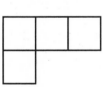
Bottom

Back

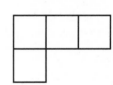
Top

2. Describe the shape of the structure you made above.

_____

_____

_____

3. Now create your own set of plans for a different structure. Then challenge a friend to build it, using your set of plans.

Patterns

Show What You Know About...

Patterns

Write a definition for the word "pattern." Then show an example of a pattern using

❋ numbers;

❋ colors; and

❋ shapes.

Can you create a pattern that uses numbers, colors, and shapes at the same time? Try it! Then explain in words what the pattern is.

DRAWING MATH

Background: Take a look around you, and you'll find plenty of patterns in nature. Honeycombs, pine cones, and the rows of corn on a cob all create patterns. Phases of the moon and seasons follow one another in a pattern. And birds traveling together often fly in patterns, too!

Directions: Look around your neighborhood for another natural pattern. Draw a picture to show what the pattern is. Or, if you prefer, draw a picture of a garden in which the flowers or vegetables are growing in a pattern that you make up yourself!

Most songs are written using patterns. Pick a song with a beat that follows a pattern. Try to describe the pattern with words.

Look at these two number patterns:

4, 8, 12, 16, 20

27, 25, 23, 21, 19

Describe how they are alike and how they are different.

Find a wallpaper or set of floor tiles that create a pattern. Use words to describe the pattern.

Describe the pattern that these shapes follow:

Then describe how the next shape in the pattern should look.

How do spies and undercover agents create and break secret codes? Sometimes they rely on patterns like this one to help them:

See the pattern? Once you find it, explain what it is and use the code to write a secret message of your own. Then challenge a classmate to crack the code and decipher the message that you wrote.

Write a few sentences explaining how patterns can be used to create secret codes.

What do checker, backgammon, and Chinese checker boards all have in common? They all contain patterns! Think of another game you know that has to do with patterns, and explain how patterns are used in the game.

Describe some of the different ways you could organize the books on a bookshelf. Which, if any, of these arrangements would you consider to be a pattern? Explain why that is.

Does your school day follow a pattern? If so, describe it. If not, explain why you don't feel it does.

September			
M	T	W	T
	1 Lunch 12:00	2 Lunch 12:00	3 Lunch 12:00
7 Lunch 12:00	8 Lunch 12:00	9 Lunch 12:00	10 Lunch 12:00
14	15	16	17

What kinds of patterns can you find on a calendar? Describe them!

What pattern do you see in these multiplication sentences? Write the next two equations that continue the pattern. Then explain the pattern in your own words.

$$3 \times 2 = 6$$
$$3 \times 20 = 60$$
$$3 \times 200 = 600$$

In what ways are the patterns found on a checkerboard similar to those found on floor tiles? In what ways are they different?

Here are three multiplication sentences.

$$1 \times 1 = 1$$
$$11 \times 11 = 121$$
$$111 \times 111 = 12,321$$

Describe any patterns you see. Then predict what $1,111,111 \times 1,111,111$ equals. Use a calculator (or a pencil and paper) to check your answer.

Imagine that your parents told you that for your allowance, you could have 1¢ today, and then double the amount of the day before every day for a month. For example, you would get 2¢ tomorrow, 4¢ the day after that, 8¢ the day after that, and so on. Would you be happy about this arrangment? Why or why not?

On a calculator, begin with a number between 11 and 19. Add 9 to it and record the answer. Keep on adding 9 and record the answers. Describe any patterns that you see.

On a calculator, begin with any two-digit number that does not end in 0. Add 5 to it and record the answer. Keep on adding 5 and record the answers. Describe any patterns that you see.

Use the One Hundred Chart worksheet on page 23 to describe the picture pattern created when you put a marker on each of the following series of numbers:

* All even numbers.

* All odd numbers.

* All multiples of 4.

* All multiples of 9.

* All *prime numbers* (numbers that only have two factors: the number itself and 1).

* All numbers that contain the digit 2.

* All numbers that contain the digit 8.

* All double-digit numbers (i.e., 11, 22, 33, and so on).

* The sum of all consecutive numbers found on the chart (i.e., $1 + 2$, $2 + 3$, $3 + 4$, and so on).

Create a pattern of your own on the One Hundred Chart worksheet. Then describe the number pattern that you made.

Marvelous Math Writing Prompts Scholastic Professional Books

One Hundred Chart

1	2	3	4	5	6	7	8	9	10
11	12	13	14	15	16	17	18	19	20
21	22	23	24	25	26	27	28	29	30
31	32	33	34	35	36	37	38	39	40
41	42	43	44	45	46	47	48	49	50
51	52	53	54	55	56	57	58	59	60
61	62	63	64	65	66	67	68	69	70
71	72	73	74	75	76	77	78	79	80
81	82	83	84	85	86	87	88	89	90
91	92	93	94	95	96	97	98	99	100

Name _____   Date _____

Square Numbers

Some ancient Greeks liked to study numbers by using shapes, such as those shown below. Note how these large squares are all made from smaller squares.

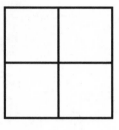 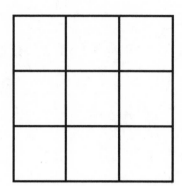 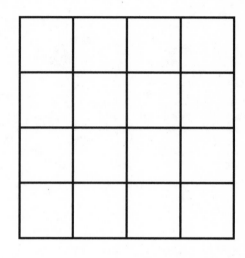

1. The numbers 4, 9, and 16 are called square numbers. Why do you think that is?

_____

_____

2. Use a sheet of graph paper to draw the next large square that fits the pattern. Then draw the one after that. Describe any number patterns that you see. (Hint: Use the One Hundred Chart and your multiplication facts to help you.) Explain some ways that you could find even larger square numbers without drawing squares.

_____

_____

_____

Marvelous Math Writing Prompts Scholastic Professional Books

Name _____ Date _____

Shifting Shapes

1. Cut out these shapes:

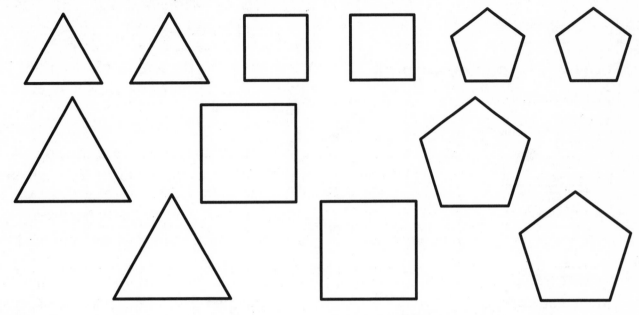

2. Color one side of each shape red. Color the other side yellow.

3. Make a pattern from four or more of the shapes. Your pattern can use ideas of shape, size, color, or number. Describe your pattern.

_____

_____

4. Now look at a classmate's pattern and describe it.

_____

_____

5. Compare your pattern with your classmate's pattern. In what ways are they similar? In what ways are they different?

_____

_____

Marvelous Math Writing Prompts   Scholastic Professional Books

Measurement

Show What You Know About...
Measurement

Explain the purpose of each of these measuring tools:

scale

measuring cup

thermometer

ruler

Now list some other measurement tools that you know. Which are used to measure weight? Volume? Time? Temperature? Length? What else, beside these things, can be measured?

A decade is an amount of time equal to ten years. What is a word for 100 years? 1,000 years? Name some other words that describe specific amounts of time. Why do you think it is helpful to have so many different "time words" in our language?

You just found two beautiful rocks, and you want to know which one weighs more—but you don't have a scale with you. Make a plan for figuring it out.

Describe one or more ways that you can measure the length of something without a standard measuring device, like a ruler.

How many measurements can you think of to describe yourself—such as height, weight, shoe size, and so on. See who in your class can create the longest list of human measurements!

Find five or more kitchen items that weigh exactly 1 pound. What are they? Are there other ways these items are all similar? In what ways are they different?

How many measurements are there on the packaging for your favorite food products? List as many as you can think of. Then look at some actual food labels and add any other measurements that you find. What does each of these measurements describe?

What measurements can you find on the dashboard of a car? Why do you think it would be unsafe for adults to drive without these measuring devices?

Describe the distance from your home to your school as specifically as you can. Then explain some ways you could make these measurements even more precise.

Marvelous Math Writing Prompts Scholastic Professional Books

When describing the distance between two cities, is it better to use units like miles and kilometers, or units like inches and centimeters? Why do you think that is?

Ben Franklin once wrote, "An ounce of prevention is worth a pound of cure." What do you think this measurement-related saying means? List some other measurement-related phrases that you've heard and explain them. Or, make up one of your own!

Would you consider a map to be a measuring device? Why or why not? Explain.

Describe a trip you have taken with your family using as many measurement words as you can. For example: How far did you go? What was the temperature? How heavy was your luggage, and so on.

What are some ways you can measure time without using a clock? List them!

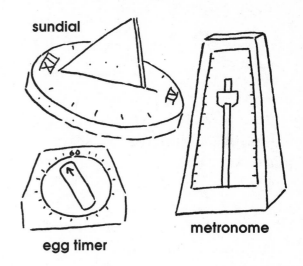

sundial

egg timer

metronome

Which do you like better, clocks with hands or digital clocks? Explain why that is.

Imagine that you suddenly grew to be as tall as a giraffe. How might your life change? Write a story about what you would see and do if you were that tall.

Imagine that you suddenly shrank to the size of an ant. How might your life change? Write a story about what you would see and do if you were that small.

Which do you think is longer: the distance around a soda can or the distance from its top to its bottom? Write down your guess, then compare these lengths using a piece of string. Describe what you find out.

Write a few sentences explaining the similarities and differences between liquid measures and dry measures. Provide a few examples of each.

Write a few sentences explaining the similarities and differences between items measured in square feet and those measured in cubic feet. Include examples of each.

In ancient Egypt, a foot was not exactly 12 inches long. It was equal to the foot-length of the king then in power! What problems might this have caused in the kingdom over time? List as many as you can think of.

Create a poem titled "How High Is Up?" in which you describe ways that "up" can be measured.

Do you prefer using metric units of measurement (like meters and liters) or standard units (like inches, feet, and quarts)? Explain why that is.

MEASUREMENT PROJECT #1

What do you think is the...

a) maximum amount of weight you can lift at one time?

b) highest you can jump?

c) farthest you can run in one minute?

Predict the answer to each question above. Then describe a way you can test your theories.

MEASUREMENT PROJECT #2

Pick a day and record the temperature outside at 9:00 a.m. and then again each hour, until 5:00 p.m. Make a chart to record your results. When you're done, write a few sentences describing these results and any patterns that you see. Do you think the results would change very much if you did it again the next day? Find out!

Marvelous Math Writing Prompts Scholastic Professional Books

Name _____ Date _____

Take a Hike—But Watch Your Weight!

You're about to head out on a two-hour hike. Take a look at the items below and decide which ones to bring. But watch out! You don't want a backache—so be sure to keep the total weight of the items down to 8 pounds or less. Then write an imaginary story about your hike.

jackknife: 3 ounces

snacks: 6 ounces

food: 1 pound, 5 ounces

camp stove and matches: 1 pound, 8 ounces

small backpack: 1 pound, 10 ounces

sleeping bag: 2 pounds, 2 ounces

first-aid kit: 1 pound, 1 ounce

maps and compass: 2 ounces

flashlight: 8 ounces

overnight pack: 5 pounds

water canteen: 2 pounds, 4 ounces

CD player and CDs: 1 pound

Items You Plan to Take	What They Weigh

(Remember: If the items weigh more than 8 pounds, go back and decide what you'll have to leave home!)

TOTAL WEIGHT _____

Marvelous Math Writing Prompts   Scholastic Professional Books

Probability and Statistics

How are pictographs like bar graphs? In what ways are they different? Explain your thinking.

Find an example of a line graph and a circle graph in a newspaper. Then describe the types of information that each one shows.

Give an example of something that you might be interested in surveying kids in your school about. Explain how a survey is different from simply asking a few people what they think.

Weather forecasters try to figure out what the weather will be like tomorrow and the day after that. Geologists and seismologists try to figure out when an earthquake may strike next. In what ways are these scientists like fortune-tellers? In what ways are they different?

Imagine that you have just created a new flavor of ice cream. But before you spend lots of money making gallons and gallons of the stuff, you want to make sure that people will buy it. Describe some things you can do to find out.

You and a friend decide to flip a coin to see who will go first in a game you're playing. Do both of you have an equal chance of winning the coin flip? Why or why not?

If a weather forecaster announces that "there is a 75 percent chance of rain today," what do you think that means? How might you use this information to help plan your day?

Marvelous Math Writing Prompts Scholastic Professional Books

Give an example of when knowing what happened in the past can help you to figure out what may happen in the future. Can we ever be certain of what will happen in the future? Why or why not?

List five or more kinds of statistics, or number facts, that are used when talking about baseball and baseball players. How else are numbers used in this sport?

Shown here is a Venn diagram that compares apples and oranges.

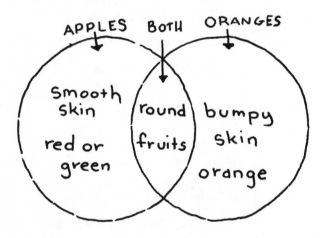

In your own words, explain what a Venn diagram shows. Then create one comparing two different types of fruit. Now add another circle to your diagram, and use it to compare three different types of fruit!

DRAWING MATH

Background: Graphs come in lots of different shapes and sizes. There are charts, pictographs, circle graphs, bar graphs, and line graphs to name just a few! All of them allow you to organize information in different ways.

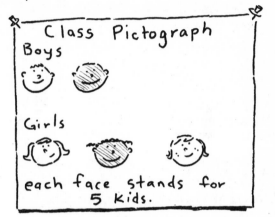

Directions: Count the number of girls and the number of boys in your classroom. Then create a pictograph that displays the results of your count. (Hint: To do it, you'll first need to decide how many kids each picture on your graph will stand for.) When you're done, display the same data on a chart and on a bar graph. On which one do you find the information easiest to read? Why do you think that is?

On TV, you may hear commercials boast things like "four out of five dentists surveyed recommend our brand of toothpaste." Can you always trust the "facts" that you learn from advertisements like these? Why or why not? How do you feel about this?

Is it possible for both of these statements to be true?

Why or why not? Find or make up another example of how statistics can be used to make claims that seem to contradict one another.

According to a television research company, the average American watches 3 hours and 46 minutes of TV daily. Does that mean that every person in the United States watches that amount of TV every day? Explain in your own words what it does mean.

Make up a silly story about a superhero who uses statistics to solve crimes and other problems. In your story, describe how your hero or heroine uses number facts to save the day!

Make a chart that will help you keep track of your money-spending, eating, or TV-watching habits for a week. Then write three or more conclusions that you can make from your chart.

You and a friend decide to take turns rolling a number cube.

✳ Each time it lands on 4, you earn a point. Each time it lands on 6, your friend earns a point. Is this a fair game? Why or why not?

✳ Now imagine playing the same game with two number cubes. Now, each time the sum of the cubes is 4, you earn a point. Each time the sum is 6 your friend earns a point. Is this a fair game? Why or why not?

How could you change the rules so that both games are fair?

You and a friend put the letters of the alphabet into a brown paper bag. You then take turns drawing letters from the bag.

✳ Each time you draw a vowel from the bag, you score a point.

✳ Each time your friend draws a consonant, he or she scores a point.

Who has a better chance of winning this game? Why is that? What could you do to make this game fair?

STATISTICS PROJECT

What color eyes does the average kid in your class have? What color hair? How tall is he or she? Take a survey to find out. Then write a paragraph comparing yourself with this average kid. How might the average kid at another school be different? Why do you think that is?

Name _____ Date _____

Let's Go for a Spin...

Think of all the ways you can roll the numbers between 2 and 12 using two number cubes. Write these on Chart #1, below. (A few are already given to get you started.) Next, roll two number cubes at least 25 times and use Chart #2 to keep track of your total on each roll. Then, on the back of this page, compare the shape of the data on the two charts. Explain why you think they look as they do.

CHART #1: Using two number cubes, show the ways you can roll a...

	2 + 1		4 + 1			6 + 2				
1 + 1	1 + 2		1 + 4	1 + 5		2 + 6			5 + 6	
2	**3**	**4**	**5**	**6**	**7**	**8**	**9**	**10**	**11**	**12**

CHART #2: Spin a pair of number cubes at least 25 times. Use "x" marks (stacked one above the other) to record what you roll each time.

2	**3**	**4**	**5**	**6**	**7**	**8**	**9**	**10**	**11**	**12**

What similarities and differences do you see between the shape of the data on the two charts above? Why do you think that may be?

Addition

Show What You Know About...
Addition

List three or more pieces of advice you would give to a friend who was stuck on an addition problem.

⊕ ⊖ ⊗ ÷ ⊕ ⊖ ⊗ ÷ ⊕ ⊖ ⊗ ÷ ⊕ ⊖ ⊗ ÷ ⊕

DRAWING MATH

Directions: Draw a picture to illustrate the following problem. Then solve it.

Problem: On her way out of Bernie's Bargain Basement, Trish counts her change. She has 15¢ left. She also has a piece of candy that she's bought for 25¢ and a pencil that she's bought for 10¢. How much money did she start with before she entered the store?

How can the equation 6 + 6 = 12 help you solve the problem 6 + 7 = ? What other addition problems can it help you to solve?

Explain how understanding place value can help you to solve an addition problem like 36 + 25 = ?

How can the equation 3 + 5 = 8 help you find the answer to the problem 30 + 50 = ? Explain your thinking.

⊕ ⊖ ⊗ ÷ ⊕ ⊖ ⊗ ÷ ⊕ ⊖ ⊗ ÷ ⊕ ⊖ ⊗ ÷ ⊕

DRAWING MATH

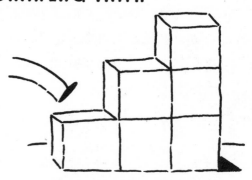

Problem: See how this stairway is made up of cubes? How many more cubes would you need for a total of 9 steps? Draw a picture to help you solve the problem. Then explain how else you could solve it.

How are the addition problems 5 + 9 and 9 + 5 alike? How are they different? Write a word problem to illustrate each.

Is it always possible to check your answer to an addition problem (such as 12 + 25 = 37) by using subtraction? Why or why not? Explain what you think.

What happens when you add zero to a number? Why is that?

Luvenia opened her math book and found that the sum of the facing pages was 243. What pages did she open to? Explain how you know.

What are you actually doing when you "regroup"? Explain.

Explain the steps you would take to solve the equation 355 + 626 = ?

Marvelous Math Writing Prompts   Scholastic Professional Books

Subtraction

Show What You Know About...
Subtraction

List three or more pieces of advice you would give to a friend who was stuck on a subtraction problem. Then explain how your friend could check his or her work.

DRAWING MATH

Directions: Draw a picture to help you solve this problem. Then solve it.

Problem: There are 12 people in a room. Six are wearing socks and 4 are wearing shoes. Three are wearing both socks and shoes. How many people in the room are in bare feet? (Hint: Be sure not to count anyone twice!)

What addition fact can help you to solve the problem 17 – 8 = ? Explain.

What happens when you subtract a number from itself? Explain why it is.

What happens when you subtract zero from a number? Explain why that is.

How can knowing the equation 7 – 2 = 5 help you to solve the subtraction problem 70 – 20 = ? Explain.

When you subtract 29 from 78, do you need to regroup? Why or why not? Explain what you would do.

Write a story about a land called TakeAway, where people know how to subtract, but not how to add.

MATH PROJECT

Stack 10 black checkers on top of a red checker. With a friend, take turns removing 1, 2, or 3 checkers from the stack. The goal of the game is to make your opponent pick up the last checker every time.

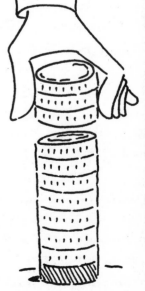

Play this game until you think you've figured out some strategies that will always allow you to win. Then describe what those strategies are!

Multiplication

Show What You Know About...
Multiplication

When can multiplication help you to solve a problem in real life? List some ideas. Then write a paragraph that begins with:

"I use multiplication when I..."

⊕ ⊝ ⊗ ⊘ ⊕ ⊝ ⊗ ⊘ ⊕ ⊝ ⊗ ⊘ ⊕ ⊝ ⊗ ⊘ ⊕ ⊝ ⊗ ⊘ ⊕

DRAWING MATH

Problem: Are there more legs on 3 ducks or 2 dogs? Eight ducks or 5 dogs? Now say you had a set of ducks and a set of dogs with an equal number of legs on each. How many of each animal might there be? Draw some pictures to help you solve these problems. Then explain how you could use multiplication to solve them instead.

What happens when you multiply a number by zero? How is this different from what happens when you multiply a number by one? Why do you think that is?

How is multiplying 3 x 5 like adding 5 + 5 + 5? What other addition problem is it like? Why is that?

About how many minutes old are you? Describe how you might figure it out using multiplication and addition. Don't forget to include leap years!

How can the multiplication problem 3 x 2 = 6 help you find the answer to 3 x 200 = ? How about 300 x 200 = ? Explain what you would do in each case.

Most guinea pigs have 4 toes on their two front feet and only 3 toes on their two rear feet. Using this information, figure out how many toes 4 guinea pigs have in all. Explain how you arrived at your answer.

While setting up a lemonade stand for the day, you figure out that you'll need 7 lemons for each pitcher of lemonade that you make. You decide to make 5 pitchers in all. How many lemons will you need? Explain how you arrived at your answer.

Marvelous Math Writing Prompts Scholastic Professional Books

Division

Show What You Know About...
Division

What's the difference between dividing 3 into 12, and 12 into 3? Will both problems result in a whole number? Why or why not?

DRAWING MATH

Problem: How many ways can you evenly group the students in your class so that no one is left out? Draw pictures to show your results. Then explain how the results might differ if one student were absent today. What about two students?

For every 5 students who get an A in math, the teacher will give the class a gold star. How many gold stars will the class get if 25 students get an A? Explain how you figured it out.

Marsha's dad made a batch of huge chocolate chip cookies. The cookies were so large that he cut each one in half. Marsha ate 7 halves. Her brother Gil ate 5 halves. How many whole cookies did they eat in all? Explain how you solved the problem.

If a number is divisible by 9, the digits in the number add up to a number divisible by 9. For example, the digits in the number 201,915 add up to 18 (2 + 0 + 1 + 9 + 1 + 5), which is divisible by 9. Thus 201,915 is, too! Test the rule using some other large numbers. Then write a rule that could help you determine whether or not a number is divisible by 10 or another number. What is it? Share your rules with the class.

Explain how you can use subtraction to help you solve the problem $20 \div 4 = ?$

What happens when you divide a number by one? Explain why.

What happens when you divide a number by itself? Explain why.

A minivan can hold 8 people. How many vans do you need for 30 people? Explain why that is.

Jamal wants to find $\frac{1}{4}$ of 20. Terry says that Jamal can use division to find the answer. Explain what Terry means.

Marvelous Math Writing Prompts   Scholastic Professional Books

Computation: Mixed Skills

How many equations can you write that describe the number 10? You can use addition, subtraction, multiplication, division, fractions, and decimals—or any combination of these—in your equations. See how many you can come up with!

When doing word problems, what clues can you look for to help you know that you may need to add? Subtract? Multiply? Divide? Why must you also read a problem carefully, rather than simply look for these types of words?

Think of a favorite book or story you have read or make up a story of your own. Then write a word problem based on the situation in that story.

Explain why you need addition, subtraction, multiplication, *and* division to solve this problem:

There are 6 dogs and twice as many cats in the window of Aaron's Animal Barn. There are half as many dogs and 4 fewer cats in the window of Patty's Pet Kingdom. How many animals in all will you find in the window of each store?

Now try and write your own word problem that requires addition, subtraction, multiplication, *and* division in order to solve it. Then give it to a classmate to solve!

Imagine that you've just started your own lawn-mowing business. Describe one or more ways that you might need to use addition, subtraction, multiplication, and division. What other math skills might you need on your new job?

Marvelous Math Writing Prompts   Scholastic Professional Books

Name ______________________ Date ______________

A Store Full of Stories

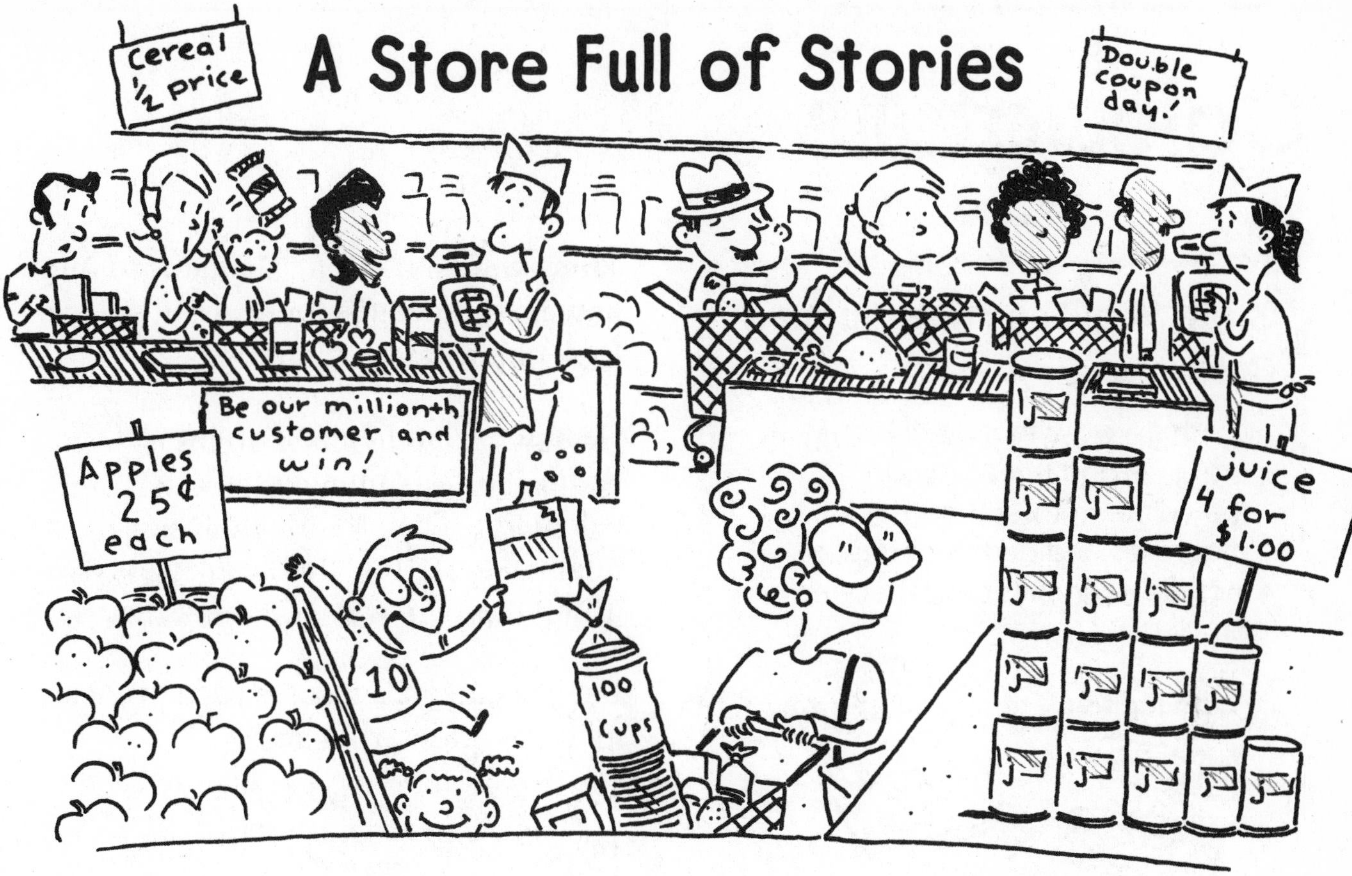

Cereal
1/2 price
Double
coupon
day!
Be our millionth
customer and
win!
Apples
25¢
each
juice
4 for
$1.00
10
100
Cups

Write four or more math story problems based on this picture. Each should use a different operation—addition, subtraction, multiplication, or division—at least once.

1. ______________________

____

2. ______________________

____

3. ______________________

____

4. ______________________

____

Calculators

Show What You Know About...
Calculators

List three ways that calculators are like—and three ways that they differ from—adding machines and cash registers. Include examples of how each one is used.

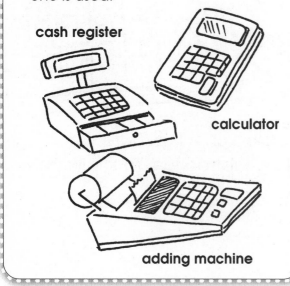

cash register

calculator

adding machine

Do you think that you should be allowed to use a calculator in your math class? Explain why or why not.

Imagine that the ⊠ key on your calculator broke. Explain how you could still use your calculator to find out the product of 3 x 1,789.

Imagine that the ÷ key on your calculator broke. Explain how you could still use your calculator to find out the quotient of 196 ÷ 49.

Jaime wants to use a calculator to find how many seconds there are in a day. Describe what he should do.

Describe what happens when you divide 0 by any number using a calculator. Then try to divide any number by 0. How do the answers differ? Explain why you think that is.

Using a calculator, solve each of these multiplication problems:

142,857 x 2 = ____   142,857 x 6 = ____

142,857 x 3 = ____   142,857 x 7 = ____

142,857 x 4 = ____   142,857 x 8 = ____

142,857 x 5 = ____   142,857 x 9 = ____

What do you notice about the products in each case? Describe it.

Using a calculator, press the ⑤ key. Then hit the ⊞ key twice, followed by the ⊟ key three times. What happened to your original number? Now clear your calculator and start with another number other than 5. Describe what happens this time.

CALCULATOR PROJECT

The next time you go shopping, use a calculator to estimate what your total bill will be. Then write a paragraph describing what happened.

Marvelous Math Writing Prompts   Scholastic Professional Books

Tic-Tac-Fifteen

Don't let this numberless calculator fool you. It's actually a game that you can play with a friend. To play, take turns writing numbers from 1 to 9 on the keys. If you're the first to get the "keys" in any row, column, or diagonal to add up to 15, you win! (Note that each number can be used only once in a game.)*

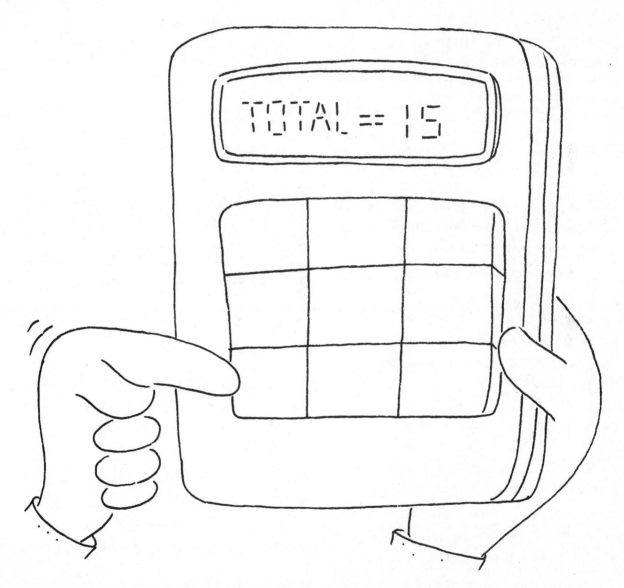

Play a few times and see if you can figure out some good strategies that would allow you to win every time. When you have some, write them down to share with a friend.

* *Suggestion: Make lots of copies of this page or ask your teacher to laminate it so that you can play over and over again.*

Mental Math

Show What You Know About...
Mental Math

Explain how the equation 9 + 6 = 15 can help you to solve each of these addition problems in your head:

19 + 6 = ?

39 + 6 = ?

79 + 6 = ?

Now explain how this same strategy can help you solve other addition problems in your head, too.

Your cousin owes you 65¢. She gives you a dollar bill. Describe how you can mentally figure out how much change to give her back.

You have $3 and you want to buy a book that costs $2.97. How much money will you have left? Explain how you know. Then imagine that, instead, the book cost $1.47. How can you mentally figure out how much money you would have left now?

In what way can thinking about quarters (25¢ coins) help you solve the equation 50 + 75 = ? mentally. Explain.

In your head, figure out how many

❅ ears are there are on 12 bunny rabbits.

❅ paws 8 dogs have.

❅ eggs there are in 3 dozen eggs.

Explain how you arrived at your answer in each case.

What is the product of

10 x 7 = ?	100 x 7 = ?
10 x 9 = ?	100 x 9 = ?
10 x 12 = ?	100 x 12 = ?
1,000 x 9 = ?	100,000 x 12 = ?

Create a rule you can always use to help you multiply in your head any number by a number that has a 1 followed by one or more zeroes.

What is the product of

200 x 2 = ?   200 x 4 = ?   200 x 8 = ?

Create a rule you can always use to help you multiply 200 by any other number in your head.

Marvelous Math Writing Prompts   Scholastic Professional Books

Suppose you found a $5 bill, 4 pennies, 7 nickels, and 2 quarters in your coat pocket. Describe how you would add up this amount of money in your head.

While using a calculator to solve the equation: 16,863 x 2 = ?, you get this result on your calculator display:

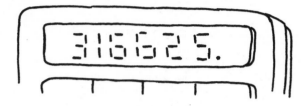

Can this answer be correct? Explain why or why not.

In your head, figure out which of these fractions does not belong:

$$\frac{1}{2} \qquad \frac{2}{4} \qquad \frac{3}{6} \qquad \frac{4}{8} \qquad \frac{5}{9} \qquad \frac{6}{12}$$

Explain how you know. Then replace that fraction with another that has an equal value to the others in the set.

Explain how you could multiply 6 x 99 in your head.

Bob says he can multiply 8 x 12 in his head. Explain how this can be done.

Hint:
12 = 10 + 2

What kinds of numbers do you find easiest to compute in your head? Explain why. Then create a list of your favorite mental math tips to share with your friends.

Explain one way to solve this problem in your head:

$$5 + 23 + 55 + 10 = ?$$

(Hint: Start with the numbers that you find easiest to add mentally. Then turn to the others.)

It's 4:12 p.m. Your mom tells you that you have 25 minutes to get ready to go shopping with her. How can you figure out mentally what time you'll be leaving?

To solve the problem 4 x 18 = ? mentally, Rebecca did this thinking in her head:

4×18
$= 4 \times (10 + 8)$
$= (4 \times 10) + (4 \times 8)$
$= 40 + 32$
$= 40 + 30 + 2$
$= 70 + 2$
$= 72$

Explain in your own words what steps Rebecca went through in her mind.

In your mind, figure out how you can make 45¢ using exactly 5 coins. How about 4 coins? Explain what you did.

Time for a Pack of Snacks

Lucky you! You have exactly $1 to spend on munchies to go with your lunch. How many different combinations of items can you buy from this machine? Note: You can buy more than one of a particular kind of snack, if you wish. But you have to do all the math in your head!

Write your possible snack combinations here:

_____

_____

_____

_____

Marvelous Math Writing Prompts   Scholastic Professional Books

Estimation

Show What You Know About...
Estimation

Imagine a conversation between an estimate and an exact number in which each explains to the other what it is, why it is a handy number to use at times, and what some of those times are. Describe what each would say to the other!

Which of these sentences contain an estimate? Which contain an exact number? Explain how you know.

✻ More than 100 people watched the baseball game.

✻ Rain stopped the game for about 30 minutes.

✻ Edna ate 3 hot dogs.

✻ The school sold 26 team shirts.

✻ The game lasted over 90 minutes.

Drop 10 paper clips into a paper cup or another small container. Now estimate about how many paper clips it would take to fill the cup. Then fill the cup with paper clips and compare your two numbers. Describe how close your estimate was, and why you think that may be.

About how far do you think it is from the floor to the ceiling of your classroom? Explain how you arrived at your estimate. Then describe a way that you could check to see if you are right!

Look in a newspaper for some examples of estimates and some examples of exact numbers. Make a chart showing these examples, whether each is an estimate or an exact number, and why that type of number was chosen in each case.

FACT:	TYPE OF NUMBER	WHY USED:
-NEWS- "More than 50,000 Crowd Stadium to Hear the Androids!"	Estimate	No one counted every single person.

You head to the store to do some shopping with $10 in your pocket. You know that the items you plan to buy will cost about that amount. Do you think it's good enough, in this case, to have an estimate of the total before you head for the cash register? Explain why or why not.

Maria estimates that 28 + 37 is about 70. Do you think that the exact answer is more or less than the estimate? Tell how you can decide without adding.

What pairs of numbers in each set below add up to more than 100? Without doing any exact computation, explain how you know in each case.

24	62	47
59	17	35
72	23	85
28	52	49

Kira estimates that 7 x 52 is about 350. Do you think that the exact answer is more or less than the estimate? Tell how you can decide without multiplying.

You want to buy a sandwich that costs $4.75 and a bottle of juice that costs $2.59. You have $8 in your pocket. Do you have enough money on you? Explain how you can figure it out just by doing some math in your head.

ESTIMATION PROJECT

How could you estimate about how much garbage you throw away every day? Create a plan, then put it into action! When you're done, describe what you learned. Also explain how your estimate compared with those of the other kids in your class.

Estimate about how many students are in your school. Then write a few sentences explaining how you arrived at your estimate and what you could do to find out how accurate it is.

Estimate the number of times you can write your name in one minute. Then have a partner time you. How close did your estimate turn out to be? Explain why you think that is.

Marvelous Math Writing Prompts   Scholastic Professional Books

Name _____   Date _____

In the Money

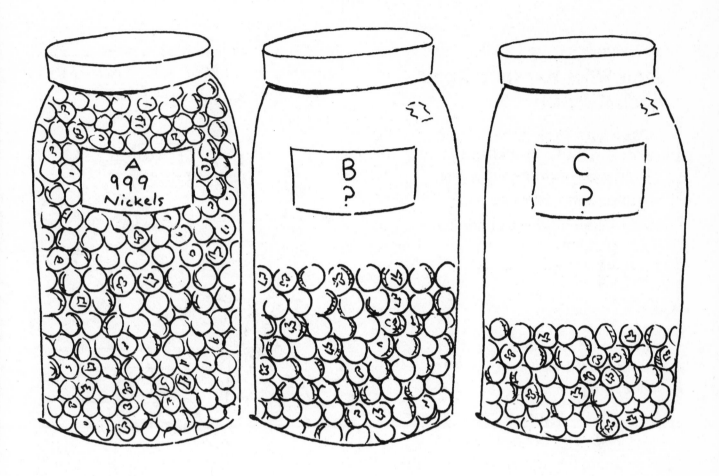

Jar A above has 999 nickels in it. About how many nickels do you think each of the other jars have? Write a sentence or two explaining each estimate.

_____

_____

_____

_____

BONUS: About how much money is in each of these jars?

Marvelous Math Writing Prompts   Scholastic Professional Books

Problem Solving

Show What You Know About...
Problem Solving

Directions: Write or find a word problem that is best solved by using each of these strategies:

  a) drawing a picture.

  b) solving a similar but simpler problem.

  c) looking for a pattern.

  d) guessing, checking, and revising.

Explain how the strategy you chose can help you to solve the problem.

This problem has information in it that you do not need: *A pet store has 5 beagles, 4 Siamese cats, and 6 dachshunds. How many dogs does the pet store have?* Which piece of information is extra? Explain why. Then solve the problem.

Write a story problem that takes two or more steps to solve.

Find a picture in a book or a magazine. Then write a story problem about it.

Mr. Cooper buys two of these toys and spends a total of $47. Which two toys did he buy? Explain how you found your answer.

Figure out how many triangles in all there are in this picture. Then write a paragraph explaining how you arrived at your answer.

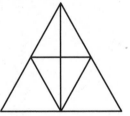

See if you can use 6 lines to draw 12 triangles. Then explain how you figured it out.

DRAWING MATH

Problem: How many different dinner combinations are there on Ted's dinner special? Explain how you arrived at your answer.

Main Course	Side Dish	Vegetable
roast beef	french fries	corn
broiled fish	rice	peas
		carrots

Use two straight lines to divide this watch into three parts so that the numbers in each section add up to the same sum. Then describe the strategy you used to arrive at your answer.

Can you find a way to arrange 8 checkers on a checkerboard so that no two checkers are in the same vertical or horizontal row, and no two squares with checkers touch each other? Give it a try! Then describe how you went about figuring it out.

Find six numbers—all of which only contain the digit 1—that have a sum of 123,456. That means the numbers you use can range from 1 to 111,111. When you're done, explain on paper how you figured it out.

Ronald takes up running as an exercise. He runs 4 miles the 1st week, 6 miles the 2nd week, 8 miles the 3rd week, and 10 miles the 4th week. What pattern do you see in the data? If the pattern continues, how many miles will Ronald have run in all after 6 weeks? Explain how you know.

Write your own story problem that has an extra piece of information in it that you do not need in order to solve the problem.

Write your own story problem that cannot be solved because there is not enough information.

Ned gets to the park at 4:00. He meets Ellen there at 4:30, and they play on the swings until 5:00. Then they head for the slides. Is there enough information given in this story problem to figure out how long Ned stayed at the park in all? Explain why or why not.

Marvelous Math Writing Prompts   Scholastic Professional Books

Izzie has exactly 46¢. What's the fewest number of coins he could have? What are those coins?

Ben buys a book for $12.99. He gives the clerk a $20 bill and gets $8.01 in change. Did Ben get the correct change? Explain why or why not.

Roll a sheet of loose leaf paper into a long narrow tube and tape it in place. Roll a second sheet into a short fat tube and tape it in place. Do you think one would hold more jelly beans than the other? Explain your thinking. Then test your guess!

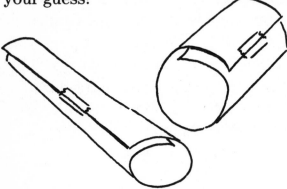

How many different ways can two people shake hands? Three people? How about four people? Make a chart showing your answers. Then describe any patterns you find in the solutions that you get.

At what age do you become a billion seconds old? Explain how you would go about figuring it out.

Imagine that you had $1,000,000. If you decided to give away $50 every hour, how long would it take you to give away the whole amount? How old would you be then? Explain how you could arrive at an answer.

Explain how three men can cross a river in a raft that holds up to 300 pounds if two of the men weigh 150 pounds each and the third man weighs exactly 300 pounds. (Hint: The men and the raft can go back and forth across the river as many times as you like.)

Sometimes if you look at the numbers on a calculator upside down, they spell out a word. See if you can figure out how to spell out the word "googol" on a calculator that's turned upside down. (That's the word for the number 1 with 100 zeros after it.) Then explain how you figured it out.

Marvelous Math Writing Prompts Scholastic Professional Books

What's the Question?

This table shows how many visitors came to two different amusement parks during one weekend:

Amusement Park	Number of Visitors on Each Day		
	Friday	Saturday	Sunday
Water World	706	924	940
Future City	668	935	851

Put a check next to the questions listed here that you can answer by using the table:

_____ How much money did visitors spend at Water World during the three days?

_____ How many visitors came to Water World during the three days?

_____ Which amusement park had more visitors on Sunday?

_____ How many people work at Future City?

_____ How many more visitors did Water World have than Future City on Friday?

Now write three more questions that you can answer by using the table. Give your questions to a friend to solve.

_____

_____

_____

_____

Part 2:
Math in My World

Math class isn't the only place students are exposed to mathematics. By the time they take their seats in the classroom, many students have already glanced at clocks, counted the change in their pockets, logged onto a computer, and played sports and other games that require at least a bit of math know-how. They've most likely come across math-related topics in books and magazines and on their favorite TV shows. And, when the school day is done, their math experiences continue as they shop, keep appointments, interact with friends and family members, practice the piano, and help prepare dinner at home. Writing about these math topics—that is, writing about math as it is used outside of school—reinforces students' understanding of the math concepts they've learned in the classroom. Such writing also motivates students to spend more energy on their math studies because as students write about math, they gain an appreciation of how math is used in almost every aspect of their lives.

Marvelous Math Writing Prompts Scholastic Professional Books

Math at Home

DRAWING MATH

Directions: Draw a picture of your family. Label the people in the picture with as many math-related facts and comparisons as you can.

2 inches taller then Dad.

2 eyes

Age 30

Age 8

Size 10 shoes

60 pounds

Dad   Mom   Me

Create a time line of important events in your life. Be sure to include the date on which these events occurred. Then illustrate the events with photos or pictures.

An inventory is a complete list of items that someone owns. Take an inventory of your own possessions (toys, games, clothes, music CDs, and so on). Then write a paragraph explaining what your possessions say about you.

Write a set of instructions that could be used to teach someone how to program a VCR, set a digital alarm clock, or use another household appliance found in your home.

Measure the area of each room in your home. Then create a chart showing the results, listing the rooms in order from smallest to largest.

Choose an object in your bedroom or kitchen. Describe it using as many numbers and math terms as you can.

Describe your dream house using as many numbers and math terms as you can. For example, how big would it be? How many rooms would it have? At what temperature would you keep each one?

100 Bed rooms
50 Bath rooms
70 Playrooms
1 Basketball Court
2 pools

How many clocks can you find in your home? What is the purpose of each one? Do you think you and your family really need this many clocks? Explain why you do or don't think so.

Why do you think clocks are built into devices like computers, stove tops, and the dashboards on cars? What are some other devices that contain clocks? Why do you think that is?

How many different ways do you use computers in your life? How do you think your life might be different if they had never been invented? Explain your thinking.

Watch as someone in your family makes dinner. Then list some ways that math is used in cooking.

How do your parents use math? Interview them about it! Then make a list of all the things your parents do that involve math.

At what temperature is your home kept? How about your refrigerator? Your freezer? Find out! Then compare your answers with those of other kids in class.

Turn on a radio for a moment. Then list all the ways you can think of that math was involved in bringing that song into your home.

Take a count of all the lightbulbs in your home. How many watts of electricity does each one use? Make a chart showing where in your home bulbs of different wattages are used.

Write a set of instructions that would help someone get from your school to your home. Make the directions as specific as you can.

Write a set of directions that explain how to make your favorite recipe.

Create a calendar showing all of the dates that are important to you and your family.

Write a poem about the importance of certain numbers in your life. For example, the numbers might include your age, address, birthday, the number of family members in your home, and so on.

What math skill do you think you use most often during the day? Explain when and how you use it.

Marvelous Math Writing Prompts   Scholastic Professional Books

Name _____ Date _____

Math at Home

Write a few sentences about the different ways you use math in your home. The pictures on this page should give you some ideas.

_____

_____

_____

_____

_____

Math at Play

MATH PROJECT

Using a Scrabble® set, answer these questions:

❋ How is math used in the tiles?

❋ How is math used on the board?

❋ What operations do you use to keep score in this game?

❋ What special squares on the board help you to score additional points? How?

❋ What is the most common letter found in a Scrabble® set? Why do you think that is?

❋ Which is the least common letter found in a Scrabble® set? Why do you think that is?

❋ Which letter has the highest value in Scrabble®? Why do you think that is?

Now create your own pieces and board for a version of the game in which you make equations instead of words. How many equal signs should you include in your game? How about plus, minus, division, and multiplication signs? How many one-, two-, and three-digit numbers? How many points should each one be worth? When you're done, test your game with a friend to see how well it works.

Name a game or sport in which the highest score wins. Write a few sentences about it. Describe what a good score is in this game and how a player earns it.

Name a game or sport in which the lowest score wins. Write a few sentences about it. Describe what a good score is in this game and how a player earns it.

Explain how your favorite card game is played. Be sure to include the rules and how score is kept.

What's your favorite sport? Explain how math is used in that sport.

Name a game or sport in which a timer is used. What is the sport? How is a timer used in it?

Think of a favorite computer game that uses math. Explain how math is used in this game.

A professional basketball team is 6 points behind. Arnie says that they can catch up by making 3 straight baskets. Ellen says that they can catch up by scoring 2 straight baskets. Sam says that both Arnie and Ellen are right. Whom do you agree with? Explain why.

How long do you think it would take you to bike one mile? Explain how you made this estimate.

Poll your classmates about their favorite games. Then chart the results and see what conclusions you can draw from the data.

Work with your classmates to create a bulletin-board display of the most amazing sports-related number facts you can find.

Work with your classmates to create a "Guinness® Book of Classroom Records." Poll your friends about their most amazing athletic feats and accomplishments—such as how far they can jump, how fast they can run, and so on. Then list the classroom record-holders in a book.

Create a game in which you need to know something about coordinate geometry in order to play. Explain the rules of the game to a friend. Then play a round of it together.

Write a report about a favorite athlete. Be sure to include as many amazing number facts and statistics about this player as you can find.

Invent a new sport that you would love to see included in the Olympics. Give the sport a name, explain how it is played, and how players would be judged or scored in this game.

Select a math skill that you have learned about in school. Then create a board game that requires this skill to play it.

Watch a favorite game or sport on TV and imagine you are a reporter covering the event for a newspaper. Write an article telling what happened during the game, who eventually won, and what the final score was.

Money Math

Show What You Know About...
Money

Write down the name of every coin and denomination (unit) of paper money you can think of and what each one is worth. List them in order of value, from smallest to largest.

DRAWING MATH

Directions: Imagine that it is your job to create a new type of coin or denomination (unit) of paper money for the United States government. How much will your new unit of money be worth? What will it look like? Draw a picture to share with the class.

If you could change the sizes, designs, and values of our coins, what would you change? Why do you think this would be better? If you wouldn't change anything, explain why that is.

Some people think that pennies are a hassle, and that the United States government should stop making them. Do you agree or disagree? Explain your thinking.

What is money? Write a definition for it in your own words.

What are some similarities and differences between keeping your money in a bank and in a piggy bank? What are some other places where people keep their savings? How do these places compare?

On what coin and bill does George Washington's face appear? Why do you think the government decided to put him on both these units of money?

How might the world be different if money had never been invented? Would life be easier or harder? What makes you think so?

What's the last thing that you bought? How much did you pay? Did you think it was worth it? Why or why not?

Marvelous Math Writing Prompts   Scholastic Professional Books

List three or more things that you can buy for 25¢ or less.

Which is a better buy: 5 pencils for 20¢ or 8 pencils for 40¢? Explain.

Make up a story from the point of view of a penny about what happens to it during its life.

When your grandparents were kids, it only cost 5¢ to ride a bus or buy a soda. About how much more does it cost to do these things today? Write a story that takes place in the future, when it costs even more to do these things or similar ones.

Do you think that it is important to check your change after you buy something? Why or why not?

Name some items that you think are too expensive and some other items that you think are good buys. Explain why you think so in each case.

What did you eat for dinner last night? How much money do you think your meal cost? Explain.

You use a $10 bill to pay for a magazine. The magazine costs $1.95. How can you tell if your change is correct?

Which of these jars of peanuts do you think is the better buy? Explain why you think so.

Pick a job you might do, such as mowing a lawn, walking a dog, cleaning an apartment, or selling lemonade. Explain how you would decide how much money to charge.

List some ways that you can earn spending money. Of these ideas, which ones would you choose? How much would you want to charge your customers? What would you do with the money you earned? Write about it!

Why do you think two different computers might have two different prices? Explain.

How do you currently get your spending money? Do you think that this is a fair way? In a letter to your parents, or whoever gives you this money, explain why you do or do not agree with this arrangement.

Marvelous Math Writing Prompts Scholastic Professional Books

Suppose you won $10,000,000 in a contest. Describe what you would do with it.

Imagine that you've just been offered $1,000,000—as long as you find a way to spend all the money within a week. What would you buy? Use catalogs, newspapers, and magazines to price the items you would want and keep a running total. Can you find a way to spend all of the money in the given time?

Do you think kids your age should get an allowance? Why or why not? If you do think they should get an allowance, how much should it be? Explain.

Which do you think is a better deal: bringing lunch to school or buying it? Explain your thinking.

"Dough," "bread," and "loot" are all slang words for money. List as many other money-related words as you can think of. Why do you think so many different ways of saying "money" exist?

What does the term "a rip-off" mean to you? Give one or more examples of something that you would consider "a rip-off."

In what way is swapping sandwiches with a friend at lunch similar to buying a sandwich at a store? In what ways is it different?

People with coin collections know that it is possible for a certain coin to be worth more than the money amount written on it. How can that be? Explain.

How are the tokens you use at video-game arcades similar to official U.S. currency? In what ways are they different?

Give some examples of how people swapped goods and services before money was invented. What problems do you think there might have been with this system? Explain.

Marvelous Math Writing Prompts   Scholastic Professional Books

Pick an item you own that you would like to sell. Write an ad in which you describe the item and tell how much you think it is worth.

Select some items from your home that you would be willing to sell in a garage sale. Explain how much money you would ask for each one and how you arrived at that price.

What do you think the phrase "saving for a rainy day" means?

Ben Franklin once said that "a penny saved is a penny earned." What do you think he meant? Do you agree? Why or why not?

List all the coin combinations you can think of that are worth 85¢. How many can you come up with in all?

Create a menu for a restaurant you'd love to open. Be sure to include appropriate prices for all of the items!

Do you know what a debt is? Have you ever heard of the national debt? What do you think it is? Explain.

Who do you think should earn more money on the job: teachers or football players? What makes you think so? Explain.

If you were to earn $6 an hour from the time you were 25 years old till the day you turned 65 years old, and you worked 40 hours a week, how much money will you have made in all? Describe all the steps you take to arrive at your answer.

If a one-fluid-ounce bottle of food coloring costs $1.59, about how much should a gallon of food coloring cost? (Hint: There are 128 fluid ounces to a gallon.) Does this price surprise you? Why or why not?

What's the fewest number of coins needed to make 32¢? What other coin combinations equal this amount?

Say you want to retile a floor that is 15 feet long and 10 feet wide. The 12-inch-square tiles that you're using cost $1.50 each. Explain how you can figure out the total cost of the tiles that you'll need.

Funny Money

What's wrong with this picture? Find as many things as you can.
For each thing that you find, write a sentence or two telling why it
seems wrong.

_____

_____

_____

_____

Marvelous Math Writing Prompts   Scholastic Professional Books

Name _____ Date _____

My Own Spending Report

Use this chart to keep track of everything that you buy for a week.
Then answer the questions below on the back of this page.

Day of the Week	What I Bought	Where I Bought It	How Much I Spent
Monday			
Tuesday			
Wednesday			
Thursday			
Friday			
Saturday			
Sunday			
TOTAL			

a. Where did you spend most of your money this week?

b. How much did you spend in all?

c. Were you surprised by how much you spent? Explain why or why not.

d. Were you surprised by the amount you spent on a particular kind of item, such as food? Explain your answer.

e. Create a plan for saving some of your money for something expensive that you want. How would you do it?

Marvelous Math Writing Prompts Scholastic Professional Books

News and Views About Math

Pick an article from a newspaper and circle all of the number facts used in it. Try to rewrite the story without this information. What do you find when you try to do so?

Do you think that either boys or girls are better at math? What makes you think so?

Estimate the number of ads (on TV, in newspapers, on billboards and posters, and so on) you see every week. Why do you think companies choose to advertise their products as much as they do? How do you feel about this?

Keep track of how much television you watch every day for a week—and how many commercials you see during that time. Select one of these ads and describe how it makes you feel.

You've just finished taking a really tough math test and a friend of yours comes up to you and asks, "Why do we need to know this stuff, anyway?" How do you respond?

What is your favorite math skill? Explain why that is.

What is your least favorite math skill? Explain why that is.

Most countries use only metric units in their measurements, while the United States uses both metric and standard units. Which do you think is a better idea? Why do you think so?

Can you think of any job or profession that does not require math knowledge at all? If so, what is it? What makes you think that no math knowledge is needed in it? If not, why do you think that math is always important, no matter what type of work people do?

Imagine a conversation between a student who likes math and one who doesn't. What would each say to the other to explain their point of view? Write a short dialogue telling what each one would say.

MATH PROJECT

Survey at least ten grown-ups to find out how they use various math skills on their job and in their life. Find a way to graph the results. Then write a paragraph explaining what you learned from the survey.

Marvelous Math Writing Prompts Scholastic Professional Books